NATIONAL GEOGRAPHIC

T0045246

All Kinds of Maps

Stevie Prince

You can learn a lot about a place by looking at a map. Different kinds of maps show different things.

The Political United States
P
Time Zones
The Political United States
Index 69

This is a political map of the United States.
It shows how people have divided the land
into 50 states.
Two of the states are not connected
to the others.

WASHINGTON
OREGON
CALIFORNIA
IDAHO
MONTANA
NORTH DAKOTA
MINNESOTA
MICHIGAN
WISCONSIN
SOUTH DAKOTA
WYOMING
NEVADA
UTAH
COLORADO
NEBRASKA
IOWA
KANSAS
MISSOURI
ILLINOIS
INDIANA
OHIO
KENTUCKY
WEST VIRGINIA
VIRGINIA
NORTH CAROLINA
TENNESSEE
ARIZONA
NEW MEXICO
OKLAHOMA
ARKANSAS
MISSISSIPPI
ALABAMA
GEORGIA
SOUTH CAROLINA
TEXAS
LOUISIANA
FLORIDA
NEW YORK
PENNSYLVANIA
NEW JERSEY
DELAWARE
MARYLAND
WASHINGTON, D.C.
MAINE
VT.
N.H.
MASS.
RHODE ISLAND
CONN.
HAWAII

This is a physical map of the United States. It shows physical features of the land such as mountains and rivers.

mountain

river

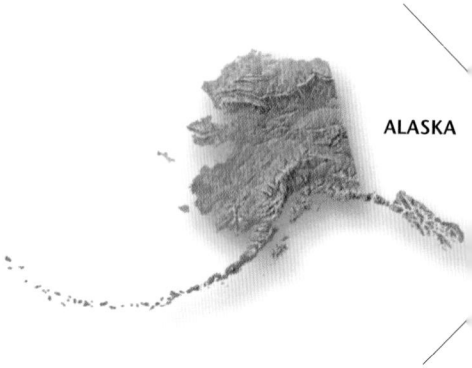

Physical Features
Mountain
Desert
Lake or river
Ice and snow
HAWAII

This is a population map of the United States. It shows which parts of the country are most populated.
Some places have a lot more people than others.

lots of people

a few people

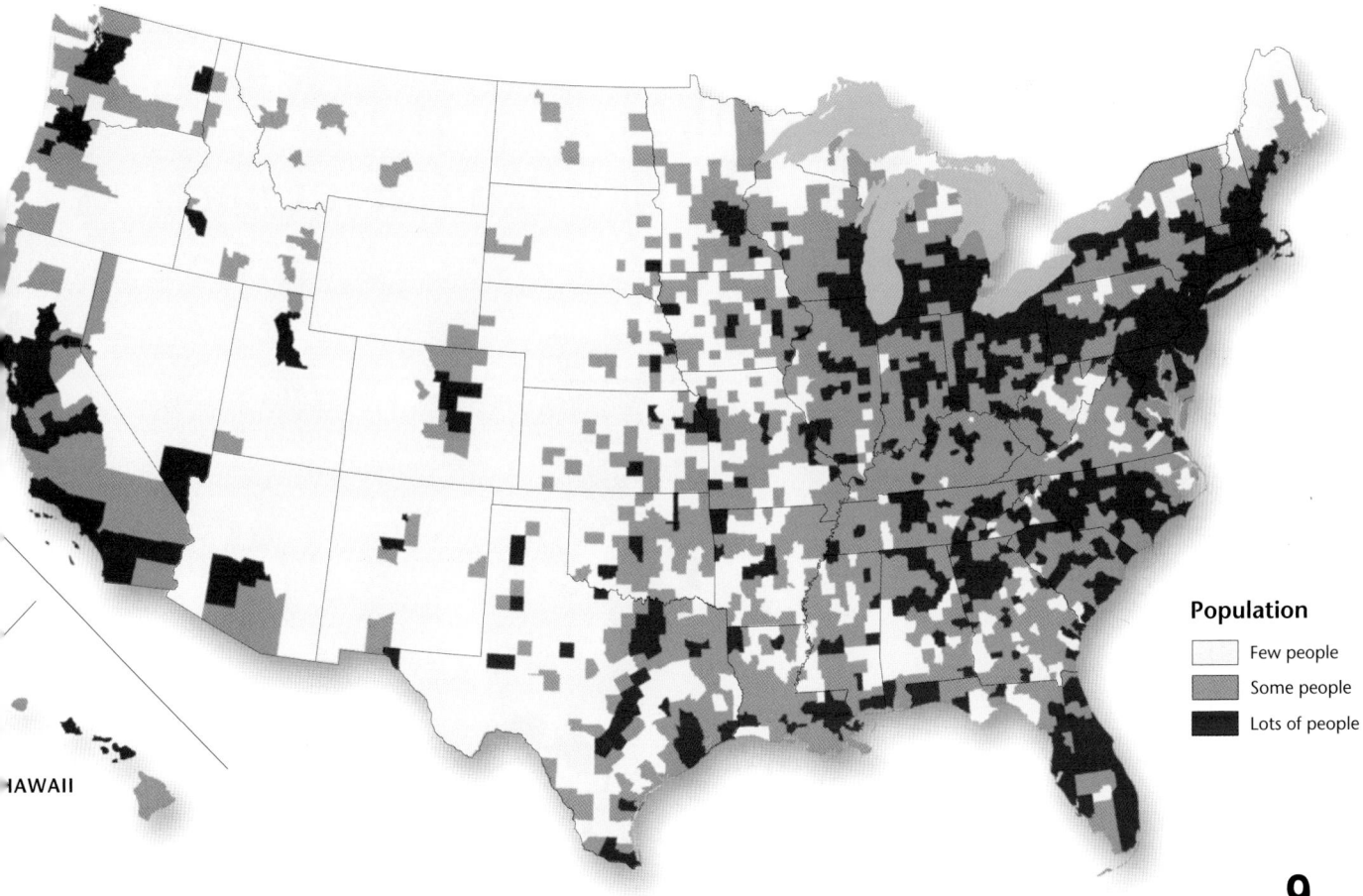
HAWAII
Population
Few people
Some people
Lots of people

This is a climate map of the United States. It shows what the climate is like in different parts of the country.

very cold

very dry

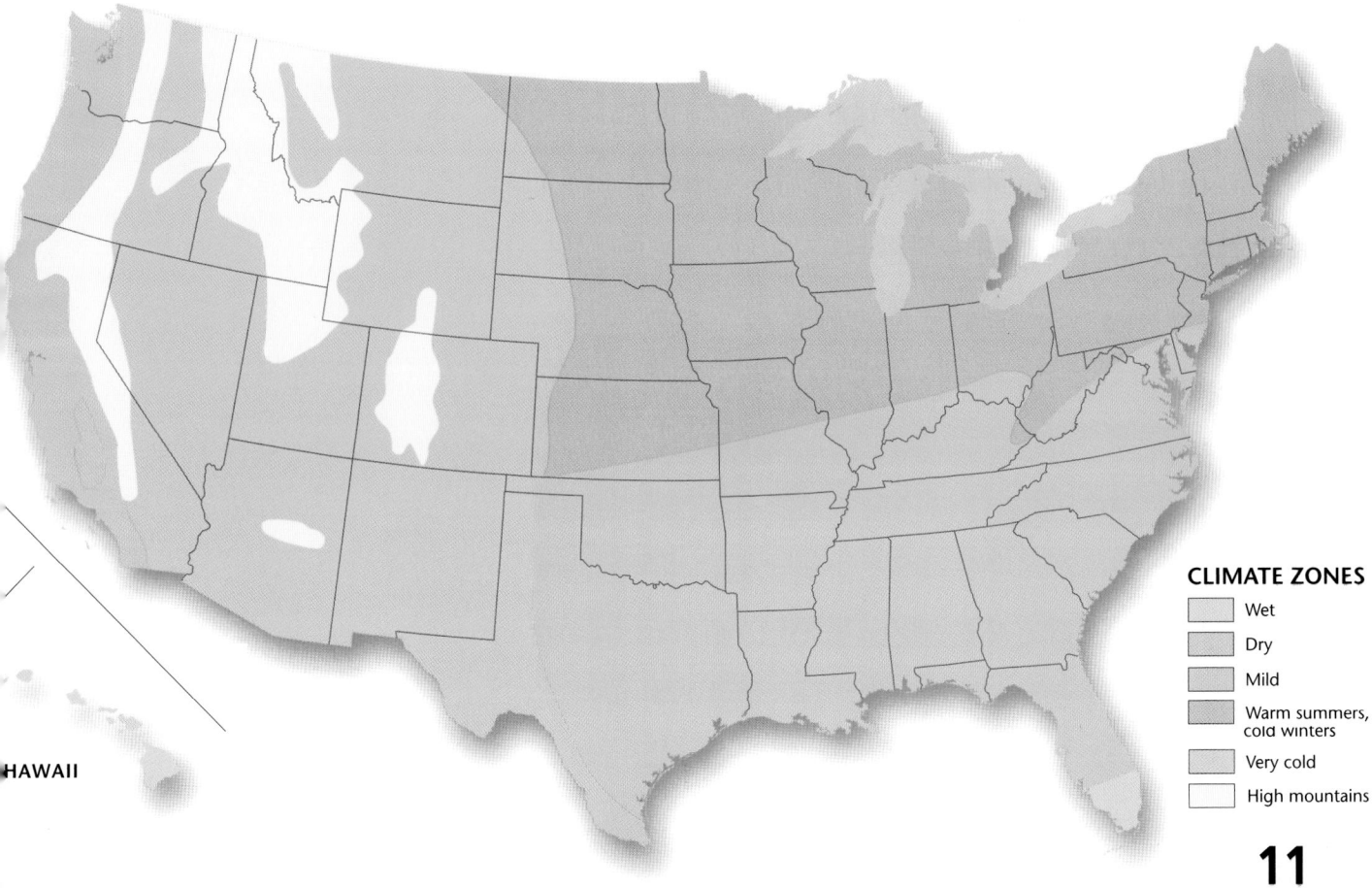
HAWAII
CLIMATE ZONES
Wet
Dry
Mild
Warm summers, cold winters
Very cold
High mountains

This is a land use map of the United States. It shows how the land is used in different parts of the country.

farmland

wetland

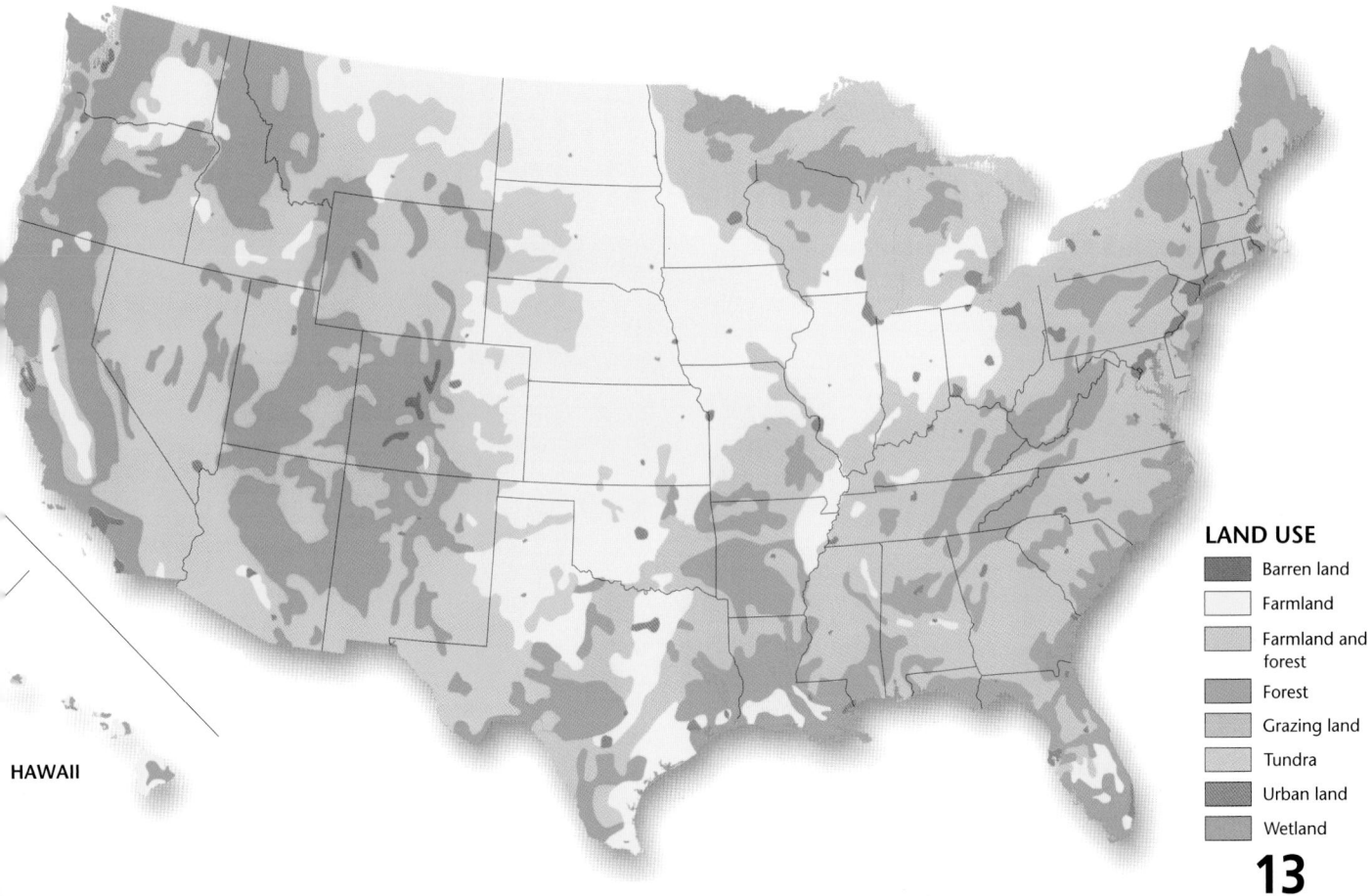
HAWAII
LAND USE
Barren land
Farmland
Farmland and forest
Forest
Grazing land
Tundra
Urban land
Wetland

This is a road map of the United States.
It shows where the major highways in the country are located.

interstate highway

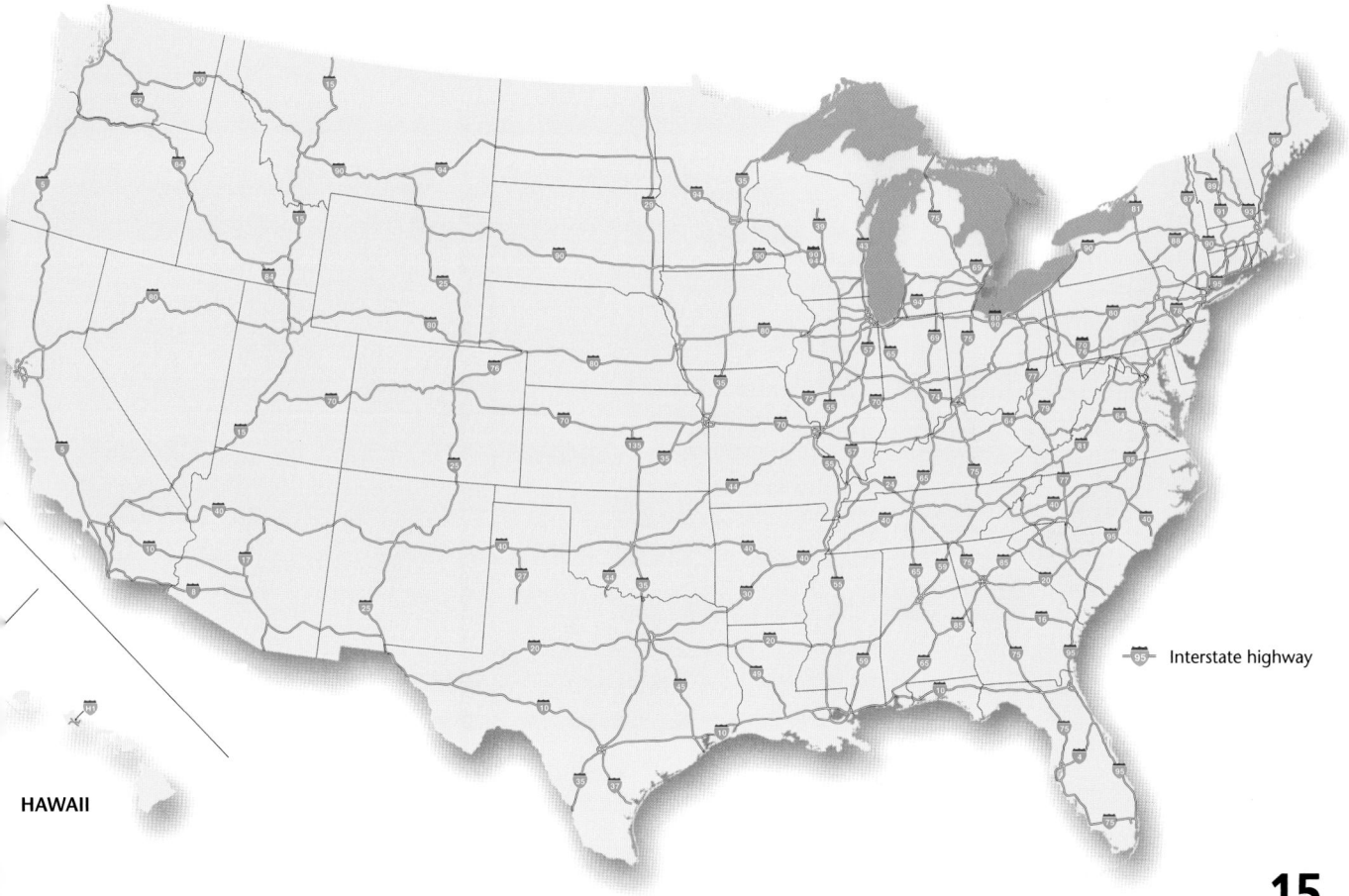
Interstate highway
HAWAII

Index

climate map 10–11
land use map 12–13
physical map 6–7
political map 4–5
population map 8–9
road map 14–15